How to Needle Tat:

A Beginner's Guide Book

by

Laura Evans

Published by BookLocker.com, Inc., Bradenton, Florida.

Printed in United States of America on acid-free paper.

BookLocker.com, Inc.
2013

First Edition

Dedication

I thank God—the first creator of beauty.
I thank my husband, Scott, for all of his support.
I thank our son, Luke, for his patience while I worked on this book.

Table of Contents

Introduction

Are you new to tatted lace? If so, this book is for you. It assumes no prior knowledge of needlework. Needle tatting is the fastest method to learn tatting. It puts you on the fast track to tat.

You'll find step-by-step instructions on how to make the double stitch—the basic stitch used in tatting. In addition, you can find explanations of techniques and basic definitions to which you may return as many times as you wish.

This is called a "Guide" because, as you learn more about tatting, you will find there are many other techniques, threads, and tools available which are not covered in this book.

Have fun exploring the many possibilities in the world of tatted lace.

Happy Tatting!

Laura

About the Author

Laura Evans has been tatting for more than 14 years. Her needlework experience began at age seven. Her grandma taught her how to embroider. Her first project was a pair of pillow cases embroidered with stem and chain stitches. Over the years she has dabbled in various types of needlework including Mountmellick embroidery, needlepoint, quilting, knitting, crochet, mixed media, and Hardanger.

Her work has won county and state awards. In 2013 she won a "Best of Show, Most Creative" ribbon at the Nebraska State Fair for her Fish Quilt. Instead of tying it together like a crazy quilt, it was tied together with tatted lace.

She is a member of the Craft and Hobby Association. She teaches needle tatting and shuttle tatting classes. She is the owner of ABC Tatting Patterns which publishes downloadable patterns at www.abctattingpatterns.com.

Supplies

Tatting Needle (Size 5)	Point of Needle ↓ ━━━━━━ ↑ Eye of Needle
Crochet Thread (Size 10)	
Needle Threader ☐1 = Bendable Wire	☐1
Small, sharp scissors	
Crochet Hook (Size 8)	
Picot Gauges: 1/2" and 1/4"	¼" ½"
Sticky Notes 3" x 5"	Start Here ↑

3

Good Things to Know Before Tatting Lace

Before you begin to tat, wash your hands. Threads absorb oils from your fingers. Oils attract dirt which stains lace. During tatting, if your hands are sweaty, use a baby wipe to remove sweat. Make sure your hands are completely dry before resuming tatting.

Crochet Thread: Choose white or a pastel color because lighter colors are easier to see.

Before you start on a large project, wind an extra 5 to 10 yards of each thread color on a plastic bobbin or a 3" x 5" index card. If you run out of ball thread, you can add the extra thread from the bobbin.

A To prevent twisted thread: Pinch ball thread between thumb and index finger. Drop needle, let it spin, and thread will untwist. Do this as often as needed.

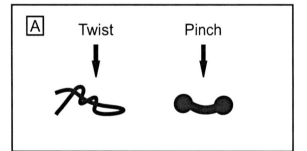

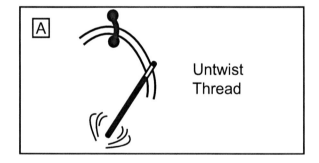

Untwist Thread

Sticky Notes

Place a sticky note under the current instructions in use. If you are interrupted, then the sticky note shows you where to resume.

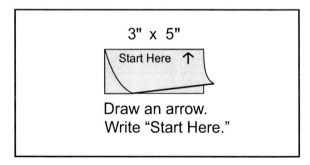

Draw an arrow.
Write "Start Here."

Thread Needle

1 Insert bendable wire of needle threader through eye of the needle.

2 Insert ⅛" of thread through bendable wire.

3 Pull out needle threader (along with thread) from the eye of needle.

Beginning tatters can pull 15" of thread through needle's eye. More experienced tatters pull one to four yards of thread through the eye of the needle.

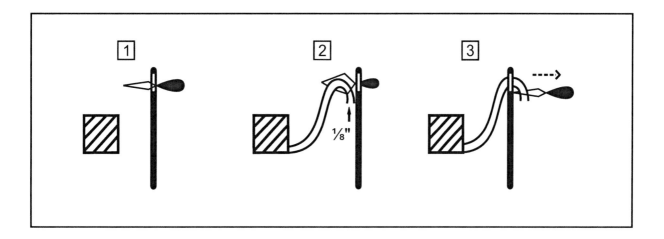

Anatomy of a Double Stitch (DS)

Cap is located above legs.
Two legs are beneath the cap.

1st leg = First Half Stitch (1HS)
 (Clockwise Wrap)

2nd leg = Second Half Stitch (2HS)
 (Counterclockwise Wrap)

Double Stitch

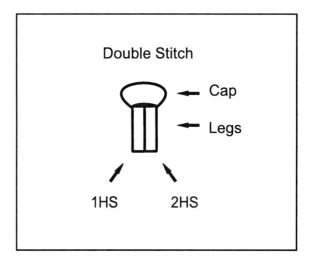

Identify Front Side and Backside

Front side: all caps are in a row.

Backside: Locate a picot, a little loop of thread. On the backside of a picot there is no cap.

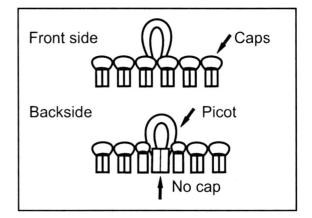

Needle Thread (NT)

A Pull 15 " of thread through eye of needle. Leave an additional 15 " of needle thread unworked before making the first double stitch. Needle Thread is also known as the Core Thread. Needle Thread has two sections: Loop and Tail End (see illustration B).

Ball Thread (BT)

B Ball Thread is the thread beyond the last double stitch on the needle to the ball of thread.

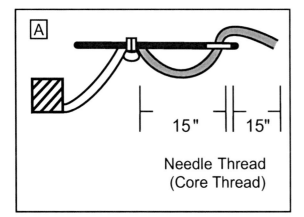

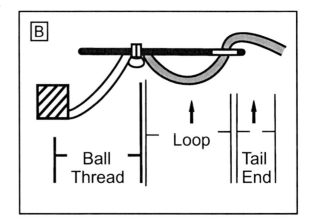

How to Hold a Needle

With right hand, hold needle like a knife when cutting steak. Place right index finger one to two inches from the point of needle. If left-handed, substitute opposite hand referred to throughout this book.

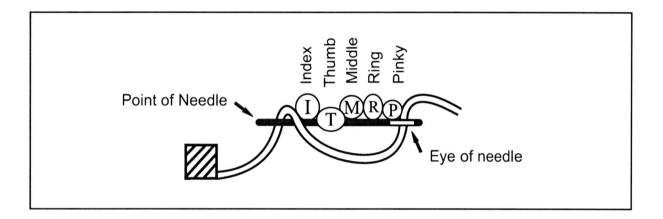

How to Needle Tat

The Double Stitch (DS)

First Half Stitch (1HS)
Clockwise Wrap (CW)

Wrap Ball Thread clockwise around left index finger. Notice ② overlaps ①.

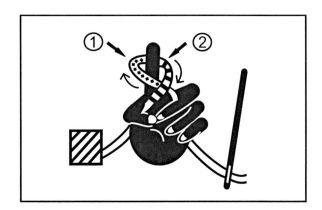

Insert tatting needle over ② and under ①.

Always insert the point of the needle toward your fingernail.

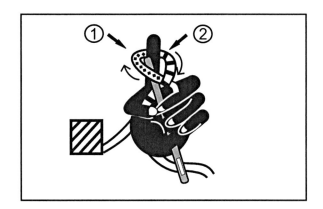

After needle is inserted, withdraw finger from thread. Use needle to lift First Half Stitch off of your left finger.

Place right index finger about one to two inches from point of needle to hold stitch in place.

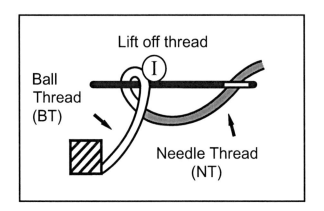

Pull on Ball Thread to snug up First Half Stitch (1HS) next to right index finger.

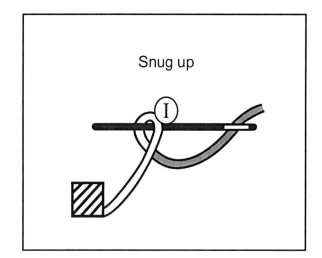

Snug up

Second Half Stitch (2HS) Counterclockwise Wrap (CCW)

Wrap Ball Thread counterclockwise around left index finger.

Wrap thread counterclockwise

A Bend index finger.
   Always insert point of needle toward your fingernail.

B Use needle to lift thread off of your left index finger.

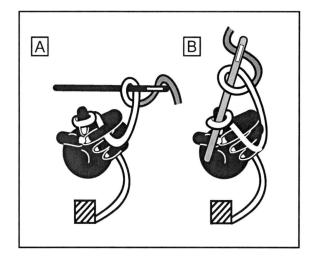

Pull on Ball Thread (BT) to snug up the Second Half Stitch next to the First Half Stitch.

The combination of the First and Second Half Stitch completes one Double Stitch (DS).

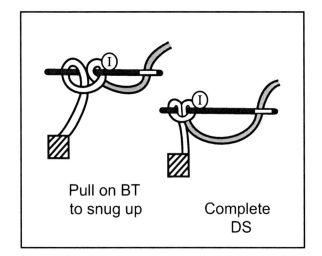

Pull on BT
to snug up

Complete
DS

A double stitch should not be too tight or too loose.

Too tight: This makes it difficult to pull up the needle through the double stitches.

Too loose: Stitches may fall off needle.

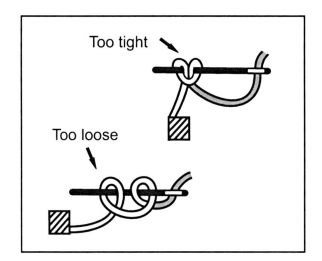

Too tight

Too loose

A double stitch should hug the needle.

The tightness or looseness of a stitch is called tension. More consistent tension is achieved through practice.

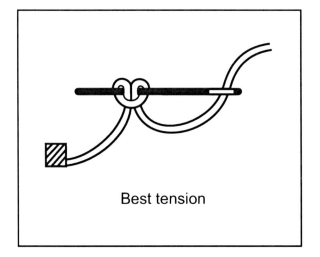

Best tension

Make the required number of double stitches according to pattern instructions.

A group of double stitches may form a ring or a chain.

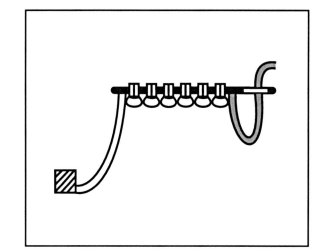

Make a Chain (Ch)

Left hand is located beneath the needle. Palm up (faces the needle).

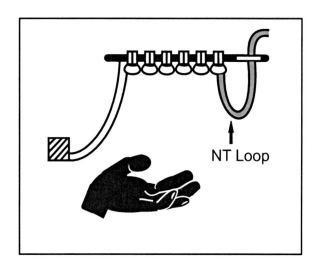

Lightly pinch last few completed double stitches between left hand (LH) thumb and index finger.

Pinch point of needle between right hand (RH) index finger and thumb.

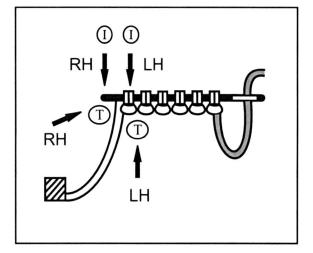

Pull needle up with right hand. With left hand, slide down the double stitches over the eye of the needle.

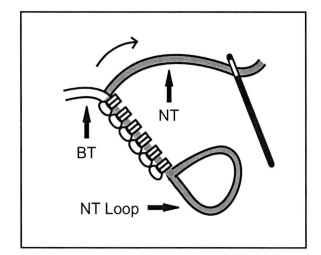

Needle Thread (NT) loop will be completely consumed (hidden) by the chain's double stitches.

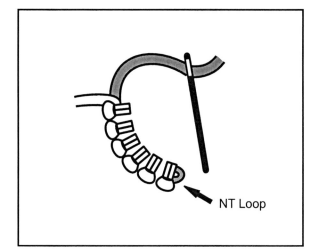

Close chain (cl.)

Turn Work (TW): Turn chain to its opposite side as if turning a page in a book.

Threads cross to form an almond shape.

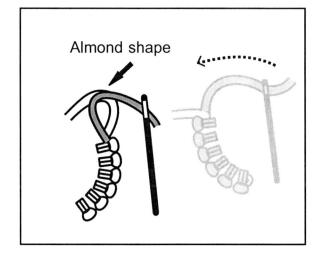

A Insert needle under Ball Thread (BT) through almond shape, and over Needle Thread (NT).

B After needle passes completely through almond shape, pull on NT to tighten threads and close chain.

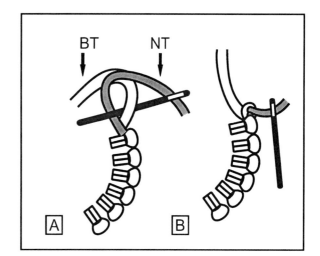

Make a Ring (R)

A Before pulling needle through double stitches, switch needle to left hand (LH). Hold last few double stitches on needle between left index finger and thumb.

B Insert left hand ring and pinky finger through Needle Thread Loop and grasp Loop.

Note: Due to space limitations, only a symbolic number of double stitches and picots are represented in ring diagrams.

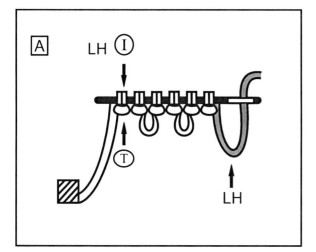

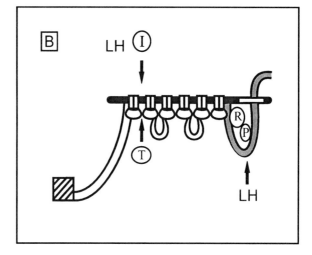

C Hold point of needle between right hand (RH) thumb and index finger. Pull needle up with right hand. The left hand slides the double stitches down over the eye of needle.

D When pulling needle through double stitches, continue holding left ring and pinky finger inside the Needle Thread Loop. It is easy to remember when making a ring use your ring finger (i.e., insert your ring and pinky fingers inside Loop). When making a chain, no ring finger is inserted in the Loop.

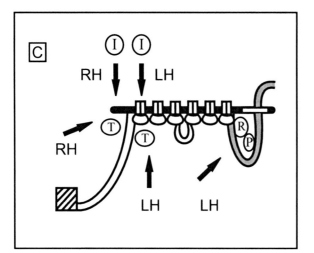

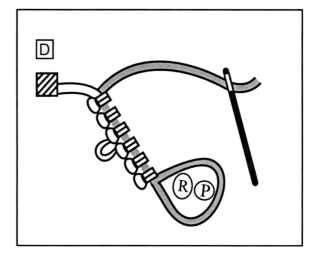

When tail end of Needle Thread (NT) passes completely through double stitches, withdraw ring and pinky fingers from Loop. Insert needle (back to front direction) through Loop.

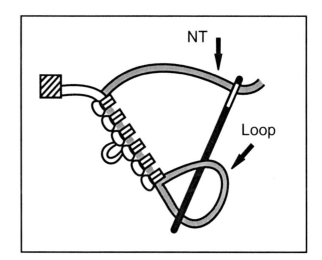

Make sure Loop is not twisted.

Twist

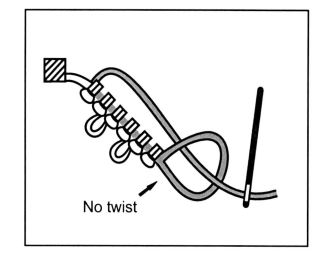

No twist

Continue to pull Needle Thread until first double stitch is next to last double stitch (DS).

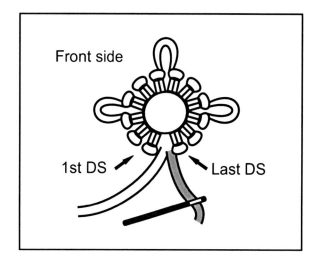

Front side

1st DS   Last DS

Close ring (cl.)

Turn Work (TW): turn ring to its opposite side as if turning a page in a book.

Ball Thread and Needle Thread cross to form an almond shape.

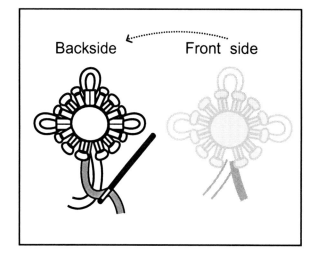

Backside   Front side

Insert needle under Ball Thread (BT), through almond shape, and over Needle Thread (NT).

See Note below.

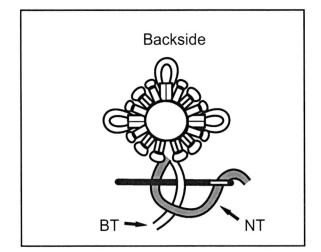

Pull on Needle Thread to tighten knot until first double stitch is next to last double stitch (DS).

This creates a circle called a ring.

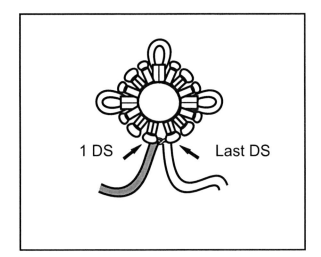

Note:
This over-under motion used in closing a ring or chain is the same as the first step used in tying a shoelace. Hence, it is also known as the Shoelace Trick. Needle Thread goes <u>under</u> Ball Thread. This creates an almond shape. Then needle goes <u>over</u> Needle Thread.

How to Read A Pattern

In the 1700s, patterns were passed down through generations using tatted examples and oral instructions. By the early 1800s, people began to write down their patterns. By 1850, patterns were plentiful and nearly every woman tatted.

There are a few difficulties in reading 19th century patterns. 1) Due to the assumption that every woman knew how to tat, often the pattern instructions did not include every step. The writer assumed you could fill in the skipped steps. 2) Sometimes writers made errors in writing the instructions. 3) There was a lack of a standard tatting pattern vernacular.

Today, pattern writers still struggle to establish a standard tatting vocabulary. This problem challenges tatted lace from gaining as much popularity as knitting and crochet. Knitting and crochet patterns have a solid foundation of standard abbreviations and symbols.

In any given tatting pattern, it is crucial to read the Abbreviation Key or Diagram Key before starting a pattern. If you don't, it is easy to misread a pattern.

Modern patterns are written in three ways: Abbreviated form
Diagram form
Numeric notation

Abbreviated: Words are used in abbreviated form. Sometimes the words are completely written out. Though, more often, instructions are abbreviated. In the later case, look for the "Abbreviation Key" to interpret your pattern.

Diagram: A diagram is a graphic representation of the design. For example, a line is used to represent a picot, and a circle may be used to symbolize a ring. The amount of double stitches used in the design is indicated by the numerals placed among the symbols. There is very little explanation given in these diagrams.

Numeric: The pattern is written using abbreviations for the elements such as a Ring (R), Chain (Ch), Josephine Knot (JK), and so on. This is followed by a set of numerals. The numerals represent the number of double stitches included in each element. The dash between the numerals represent a picot. Numeric notation has very little supplementary material. A basic tatting knowledge is required to read this type of pattern.

The following *Little Lace Flower* pattern is completely written out. It tells a beginning tatter all the things she needs to remember while tatting. Examples of the above three forms are given after the fully written out instructions. If you have trouble reading any form, go back to the written instructions. Put the challenging form next to the written instructions and alternate between reading the written instructions and reading the challenging pattern form.

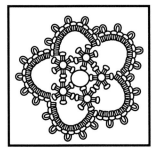

Little Lace Flower

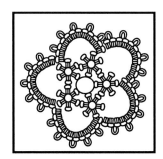

<u>Supplies</u>

Crochet Thread (Size 10)
Crochet Hook (Size 8)
Tatting Needle (Size 5)
Needle Threader
Small, sharp scissors
Picot Gauge 1/2"
Picot Gauge 1/4"

<u>Optional Supplies</u>

Magnifying glasses (to see thread)
3" x 5" sticky note
    (Place sticky note under
    current instructions to help
    keep track of your place.)

Pinning Board (See page 54.)

Starting Row

☐ **Ring:** Make 3 double stitches, picot (use ½" picot gauge), 3 double stitches. Close ring. To make a double stitch, see page 8. To use a picot gauge, see page 43.

How to Close Ring

A Start with left hand beneath needle. With left thumb and index finger, pinch last double stitch made on needle. Insert left ring finger Ⓡ and pinky Ⓟ through Needle Thread Loop. ("Needle Thread Loop" is also referred to as the "Loop.")

B With right hand pinch, pull needle up. With left hand pinch, slide down double stitches over eye of needle. Continue holding Loop open with left ring and pinky finger.

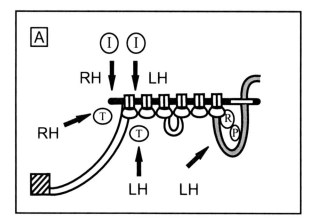

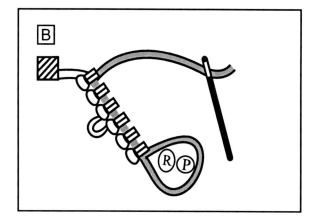

C When tail of the Needle Thread completely passes through double stitches, withdraw fingers from Loop. Make sure Loop is not twisted. Insert needle (from back to front direction) through Loop. Pull on the Needle Thread until the first double stitch is next to the last double stitch.

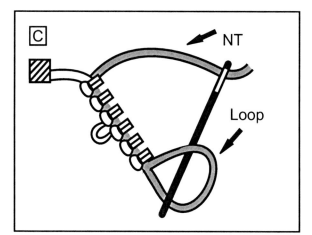

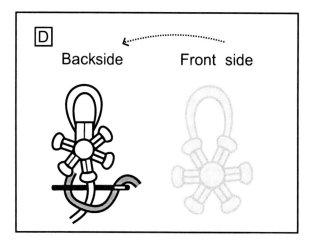

D Turn work to its opposite side as if turning a page in a book (right to left). An almond shape forms when the Needle Thread crosses over the Ball Thread. Insert needle under Ball Thread and through almond shape. To tighten, pull Ball Thread and Needle Thread in opposite directions.

Track your progress: place a checkmark in box next to "Ring" on page 18.

Laura Evans

| A | **Set Up for First Chain**

Turn ring so front side faces you.

Center picot points to ceiling. |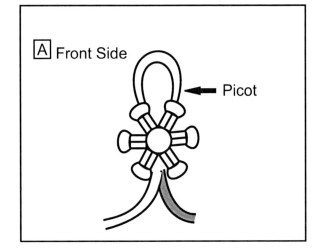

A Front Side — Picot |

| B | Reverse work to its opposite side.

To do this, pinch center picot between right thumb and index finger. Flip ring to its opposite side as if opening an oven door. |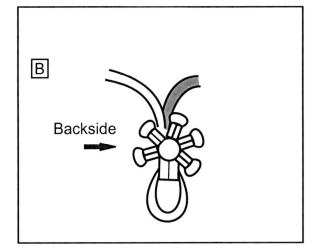

B Backside |

| C | Place needle on top of last double stitch of ring. |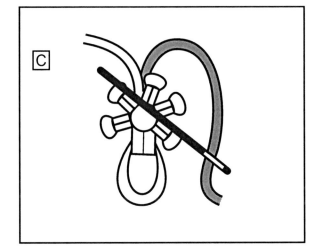

C |

20

A | Make first double stitch of the chain.

To avoid a gap between a ring and a chain, make sure needle is on top of last double stitch. Pull on Ball Thread to snug up the First Half Stitch of chain next to last double stitch of ring. Then secure First Half Stitch by placing right index finger on top of it. Make Second Half Stitch of double stitch and snug up.

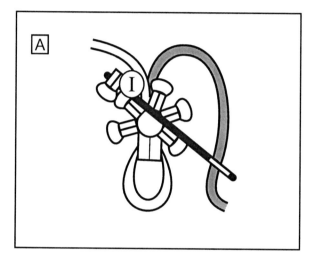

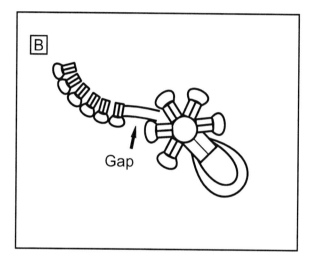

Gap

B | If first double stitch is not close enough to last double stitch of the ring, you will get a gap.

You have completed the first double stitch of the chain. Continue following pattern instructions below. You will begin by making the second double stitch.

☐ Chain: 2 double stitches, picot (¼") [All remaining picots use ¼" picot gauge.]
        2 double stitches, picot,
        2 double stitches, picot,
        2 double stitches, picot,
        2 double stitches, picot,
        2 double stitches. Close chain.

Close Chain

A With right hand index finger and thumb pull needle up. Use left hand to slide down double stitches over eye of needle. (Due to space limitations, only a symbolic number of double stitches and picots are represented in chain diagrams.)

B Turn work to its opposite side as if turning a page in a book. Front side faces you. Needle Thread (NT) is on top of Ball Thread. An almond shape forms when these two threads cross. Insert needle under Ball Thread (BT) through almond shape. Pull Ball and Needle threads in opposite directions to tighten knot.

<u>Track your progress:</u> place a checkmark in the box next to "Chain" on page 21.

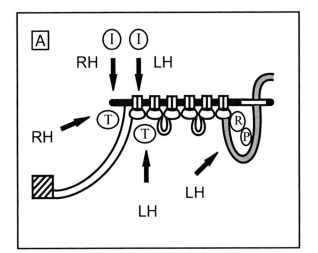

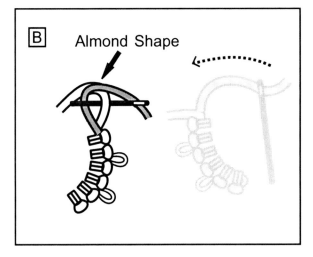

Orientation of Ball Thread in this pattern: whenever the front side faces you, the Ball Thread is always on the left side of work.

Keep track of your work: Each time you complete a ring, put a checkmark in one box next to "Ring" on page 23. Each time you complete a chain, put a checkmark in one box next to "Chain" on page 26.

Continue following the remaining instructions. Repeat the ring and chain pattern four times.

☐ ☐ ☐ ☐ **Ring**: Make 3 double stitches.
Join: Front side faces you. Center picot of first ring points to ceiling.

Lay Ball Thread across the top of center picot made in first ring.

A right side Ⓐ and left side Ⓑ of the picot becomes apparent.

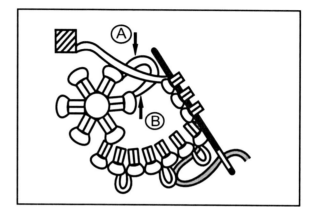

Ⓑ With left thumb and index finger, pinch picot and Ball Thread. Continue holding this pinch while inserting needle on the right side and from beneath the picot. Slightly lift thumb. Then slide needle on top of Ball Thread. Use needle to push Ball Thread down through picot.

Ⓒ Pull up needle. The Ball Thread sits correctly oriented on needle. Note: you can use a crochet hook instead of a tatting needle to make a join.

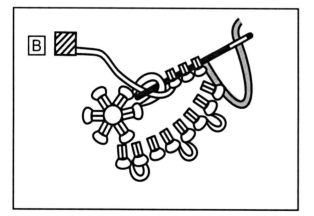

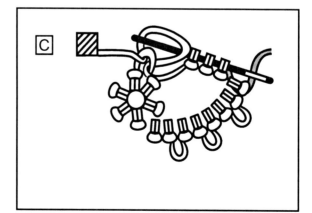

[D] Pull on Ball Thread to snug up Join. This single stitch is called a Join.

Finish ring: Make 3 double stitches. Close ring.

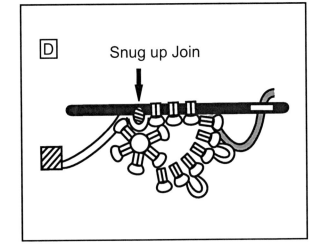

[D] Snug up Join

[A] Close A Ring:

Pinch point of needle with right thumb and index finger. Pull needle up and slide the double stitches down over the eye of needle.

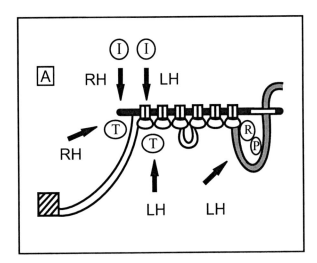

[A] RH   LH   (I) (I)   RH   (T) (T)   LH   LH   (R)(P)

[B] Continue holding needle's Loop open with left ring finger until tail end of Needle Thread passes completely through double stitches.

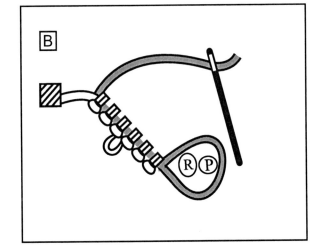

[B] (R)(P)

C | Withdraw fingers from Loop. Insert needle and Needle Thread completely through Loop. Front side is facing you. Pull on Needle Thread to close ring.

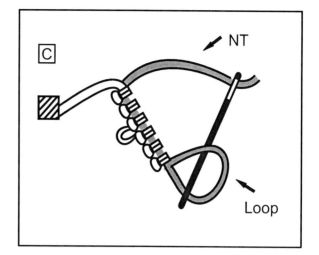

D | Turn work to its opposite side as if turning a page. This forms an almond shape.

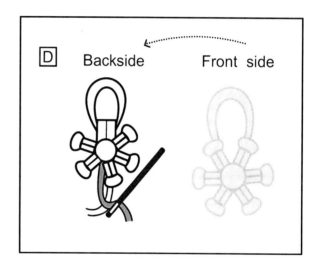

E | Insert needle under Ball Thread (BT), through almond shape, and over Needle Thread (NT). Tighten knot. Let needle dangle to untwist thread.

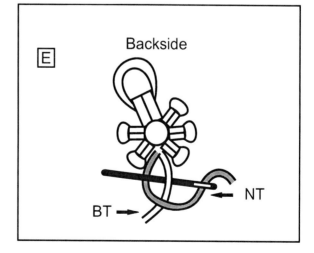

□□□□ **Chain:** 2 double stitches, picot (¼")
2 double stitches, picot,
2 double stitches, picot,
2 double stitches, picot,
2 double stitches, picot,
2 double stitches.
Close chain.

Ⓐ Backside faces you. Place needle on top of last double stitch of last completed ring. Use Ball Thread to make a chain.

Remember to snug up First and Second Half Stitch to avoid gapsosis.

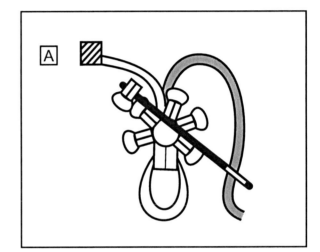

Ⓐ **Close Chain:**

Backside faces you. Lightly pinch last double stitch on needle between left thumb and index finger. With right hand, pinch the point of needle and pull needle up. With left hand, slide the double stitches down over the eye of the needle.

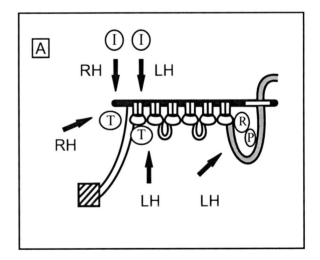

B When making a chain, do not insert any fingers inside of Loop. Just pull Needle Thread through double stitches. Loop will be consumed by the chain.

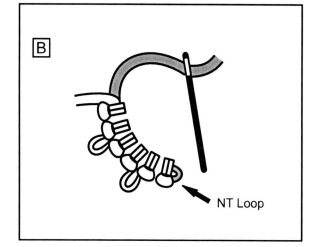

B

NT Loop

C Turn work (e.g., chain) to its opposite side as if turning a page. Now the front side faces you. An almond shape is formed. Insert needle under Ball Thread (BT), through almond shape, and over Needle Thread. Pull Ball Thread and Needle Thread in opposite directions to tighten knot.

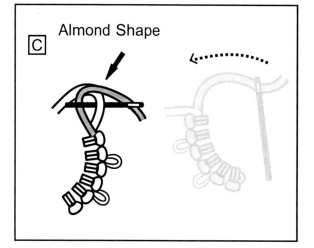

Almond Shape

C

Begin with the "Starting Row," then repeat the ring and chain pattern four times. The pattern is complete when there are a total of five rings and five chains.

Remember to place a checkmark in the box next to "Ring" or "Chain" each time you complete a ring or chain. If you are interrupted, go back to your sticky note or checkmark to see where to resume tatting.

Finish

After the last chain is completed, leave 3" of Ball Thread and 3" of Needle Thread before cutting off these threads. Backside of lace faces you. Insert crochet hook (floor to ceiling direction) in the space between the closure of the first ring and closure of the first chain. Catch one tail end with crochet hook and pull tail end through to the backside. Tie tail ends in a square knot.

See "Reference" at www.abctattingpatterns.com for a video on how to make a square knot.

Little Lace Flower

Abbreviated Form

Abbreviation Key

DS   = Double Stitch
Ch   = Chain
Cl   = Close
P / – = Picot
RODS = Reverse Order of Double Stitches (Counterclockwise / Clockwise Wrap)
RW   = Reverse Work to its opposite side as if flipping down an oven door
R   = Ring
TW   = Turn work to its opposite side as if turning a page in a book
+   = Join to picot

½ " = Center picot
¼ " = All other picots

R: 3 ds, p (½"), 3 ds. RW. Cl.
Ch (RODS): 2 ds, p (¼"), 2 ds, p, 2 ds, p, 2 ds, p, 2 ds, p, 2 ds. TW. Cl.

*R: 3 ds, + (join to center picot), 3 ds. TW. Cl.
Ch (RODS): 2 ds, p (¼"), 2 ds, p, 2 ds, p, 2 ds, p, 2 ds, p, 2 ds. TW. Cl.*

Repeat 4 more times from * to *.
Leave 3" tails. Insert one tail through closure of first chain. Tie tails in a square knot.

Numeric Notation

R: 3 - 3. RW. Cl.
Ch (RODS): 2 - 2 - 2 - 2 - 2 - 2. TW. Cl.

*R: 3 + 3. TW. Cl.
Ch (RODS): 2 - 2 - 2 - 2 - 2 - 2. TW. Cl.* (4x)

Leave 3" tails. Insert one tail through closure of first chain.
Tie tails in a square knot.

Diagram Form

Diagram Key

Start at "A"

| = Picot (1/4")

O = Center Picot (1/2")

⌒ = Chain

ᴅ = Ring

Numerals = Number of DS

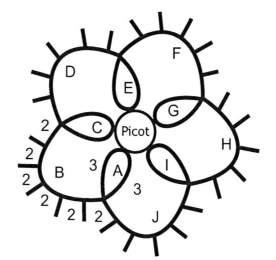

Basic Techniques and Definitions

Add New Thread

Adding new thread takes several steps. The best place to add new thread is in the space between last completed ring and chain.

First secure old thread in the following manner.

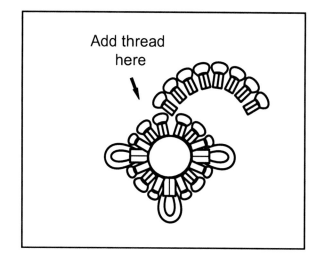

Add thread here

A On backside of last ring, insert needle through last three stitches.

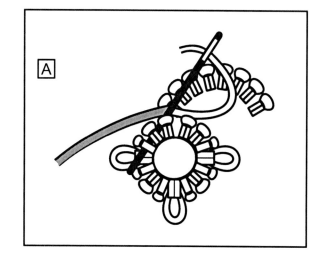

A

B Pull through old Ball Thread.

① Tail end of white Ball Thread is buried beneath these three stitches.

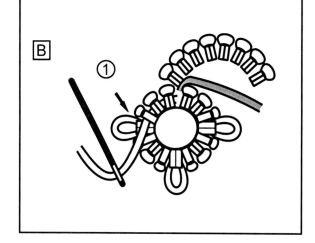

B

①

C Skip two stitches and insert needle in the opposite direction of previous insertion.

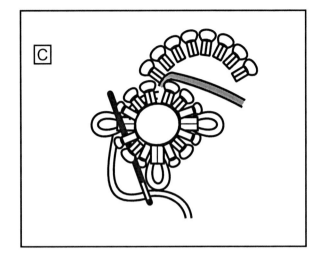

D Pull old Ball Thread through those two double stitches. Pull tight. Cut old ball thread.

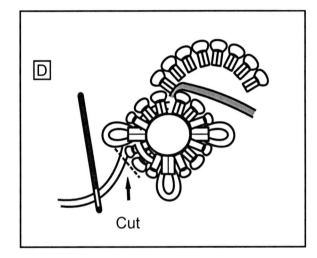

Cut

E Leave 8" of Needle Thread. Then cut Needle Thread.

Rethread needle with 8" of Needle Thread (NT).

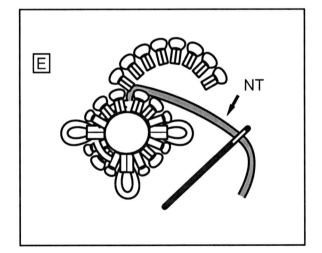

NT

F Backside of ring faces you. Insert needle on opposite side of ring.

Repeat instructions A though D to hide Needle Thread.

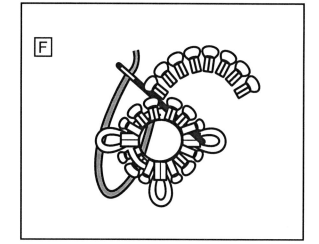

F

G All old thread is hidden beneath double stitches.

Now you are ready to add new thread.

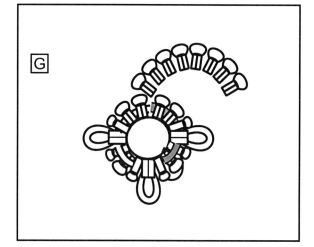

G

H Thread needle with new thread. If you are out of the original Ball Thread, use the 5 - 10 yards wound on a plastic bobbin or index card.

Pull about 15" of new thread through needle's eye. Leave 15" of thread before making first double stitch.

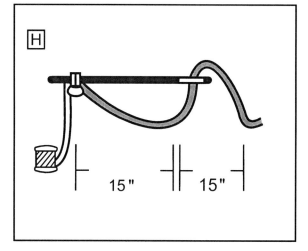

H

I Front side of last ring faces you. Insert needle (front to back direction) through left side at the base of chain. Pull through Needle Thread and its tail to the backside.

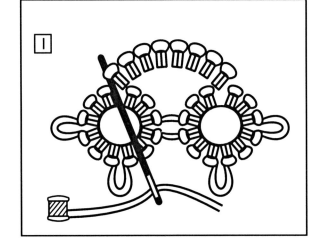

J Turn work as if turning a page in a book. Backside faces you.

Close thread using the Shoelace Trick (see page 51).

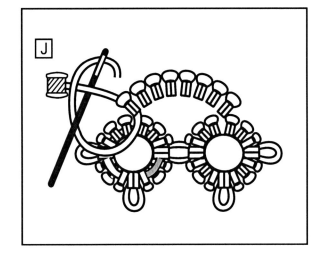

K Backside faces you. Ball Thread (BT) is behind last completed ring. Needle Thread (NT) is in front of last completed ring.

Use new Ball Thread to make the number of double stitches per pattern instructions.

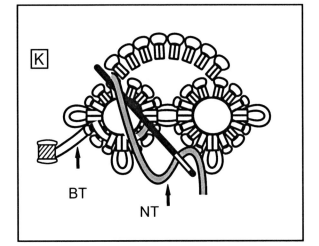

Bare Thread Space (BTS)

Leave an unworked length of Needle Thread, i.e., Needle Thread without double stitches.

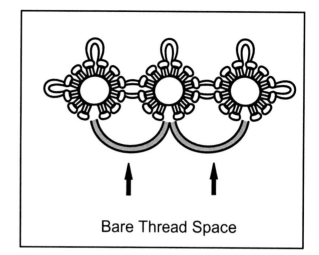

Bare Thread Space

To make uniform lengths of Bare Thread Space (BTS) measure BTS with a ruler or a picot gauge (see page 43).

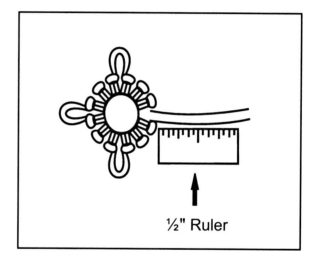

½" Ruler

Correct Errors

Slide off offending stitch and the stitches in front of the offending stitch.

The example at right shows three stitches will be removed from the needle.

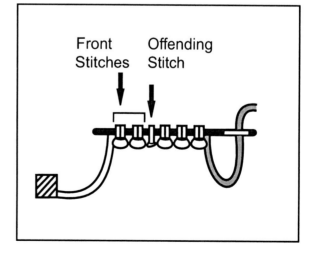

Front Stitches   Offending Stitch

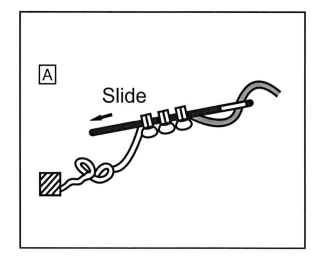

⟨A⟩ Slide off the three offending stitches.

⟨A⟩ **Slide**

⟨B⟩ Add three new double stitches.

Continue tatting per pattern instructions.

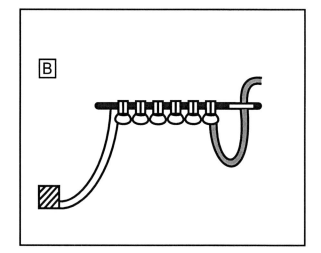

⟨B⟩

<u>Cut & Tie Threads (C&T)</u>

Leave 3" tail ends of Ball Thread (BT) and Needle Thread (NT) before cutting.

Tie tails in a square knot (see page 52).

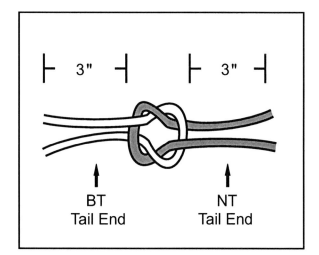

├ 3" ┤   ├ 3" ┤

BT Tail End   NT Tail End

36

Element

An element is any technique or stitch which contributes to the art of tatting. Basic elements include a ring, chain, and a picot. In addition, it includes such knots as the square knot and slip knot. Also, it includes any manipulated double stitch to form a corollary stitch such as the Josephine Chain or Josephine Knot (see pages 41-42).

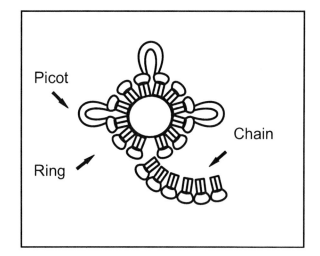

Flawless Front (FF)

All caps face front like a row of birds sitting on a wire.

Backside: Locate picot. The backside of a picot does not have a cap.

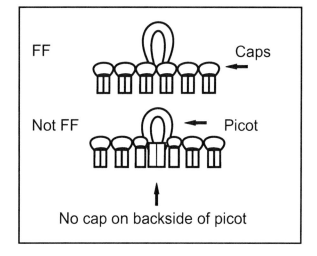

To make a Flawless Front (FF):

When front side of lace faces you, make new double stitches in normal order: clockwise wrap / counterclockwise wrap.

When backside faces you, make new double stitches in reverse order: counterclockwise wrap / clockwise wrap (RODS).

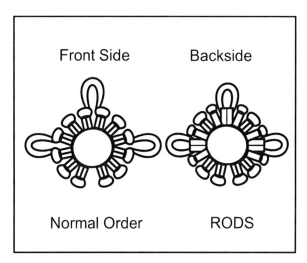

Gapsosis

Gaps weaken tatted lace.

A gap occurs when an unworked section of thread is left between two elements such as a ring and a chain.

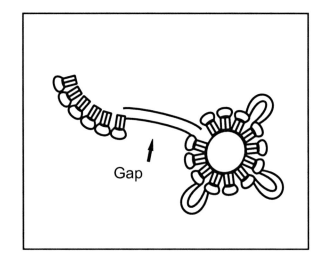

Gap

Prevent Gapsosis

Place needle on top of last completed double stitch.

Make First Half Stitch of chain. Pull on Ball Thread to snug it up next to last double stitch of ring. Hold index finger on top of this stitch. Make Second Half Stitch and snug up.

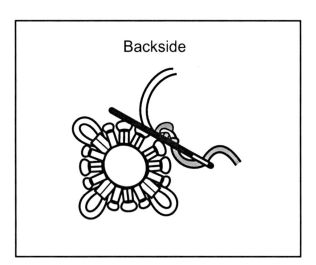

Backside

Join to Picot (J or + or ±)

Joins are made between a previously made picot (old picot) and a new picot.

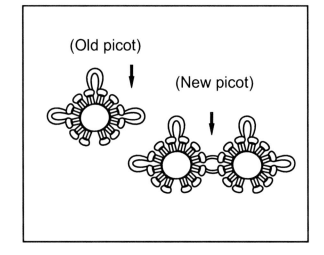

(Old picot)

(New picot)

A **To make a Join:**

Lay Ball Thread across the top of picot.

A right side Ⓐ and left side Ⓑ of the picot becomes apparent.

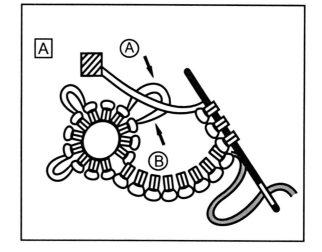

B Insert crochet hook from beneath picot (on the right side of picot), through front of picot and over Ball Thread. Pull crochet hook and Ball Thread in a downward motion.

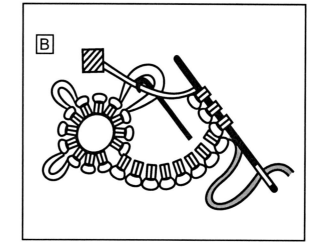

C Continue pulling crochet hook until a loop is formed.

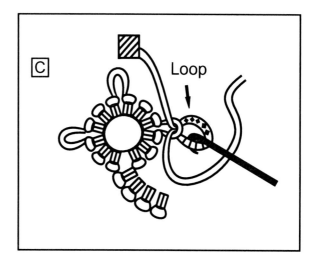

Loop

D When pulling Ball Thread through picot, do not twist crochet hook as it will create a twisted loop.

Also, if loop is placed incorrectly on the needle, it will result in a twisted stitch.

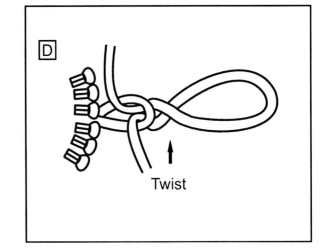

E Use a crochet hook to place loop on needle. Part ② of loop is placed in front of needle.

Part ① of loop is placed behind needle. Pull on Ball Thread to snug up join.

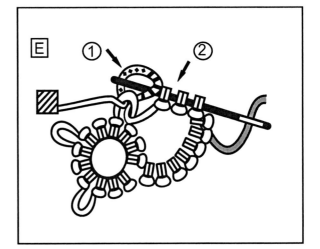

Join: How to Count

Some pattern writers count a joined picot as one stitch because the joining thread adds thickness and takes up space.

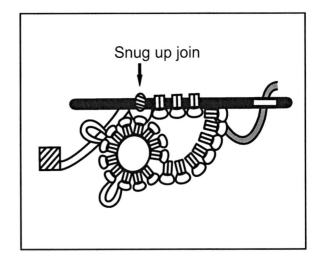

Other pattern writers count a Join as zero (i.e., do not count the Join as one stitch.)

Follow the instructions of each pattern writer.

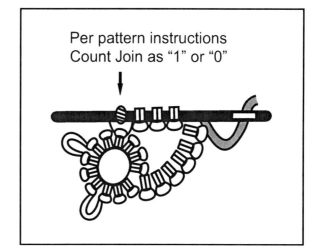

Per pattern instructions
Count Join as "1" or "0"

Picot: Not Joined

If a picot is not joined, then that picot, (A) , is always counted as zero.

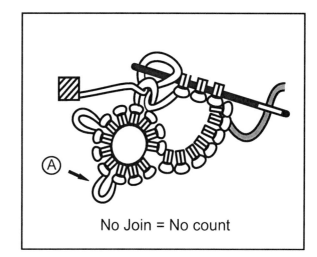

No Join = No count

Josephine Chain (JC)

Use only the Second Half Stitch of double stitch (counterclockwise wrap). Each Second Half Stitch is counted as one stitch.

Repeat counterclockwise wrap
12 times

Close as a normal chain.
The stitches will form a spiral.

Sometimes, a Josephine Chain is
called a Josephine Spiral.

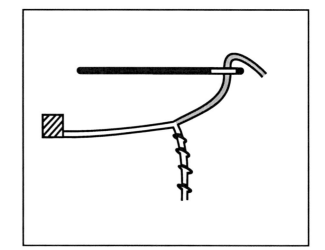

Josephine Knot (JK)

Use only the Second Half Stitch of the
double stitch (counterclockwise wrap).
Each Second Half Stitch is counted as
one stitch.

In this example: Repeat Second Half
Stitch (counterclockwise wrap) ten
times.

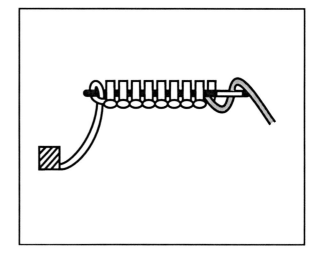

Close as you would close a normal
ring.

A Josephine Knot lays flatter than a
ring made of normal double stitches.

Picot (P or — or ⍟ or ±)

After last double stitch, Ⓐ, leave a Bare Thread Space by placing right index finger, Ⓘ , a little beyond last double stitch. Make First and Second Half Stitch. Snug up each Half against index finger.

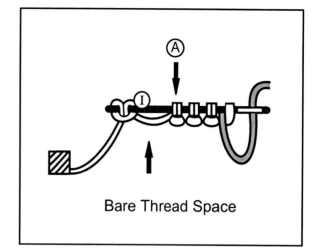

Bare Thread Space

Remove index finger.

Slide new double stitch Ⓑ against previous double stitch Ⓒ.

Sliding Ⓑ against Ⓒ makes the Bare Thread Space form a picot.

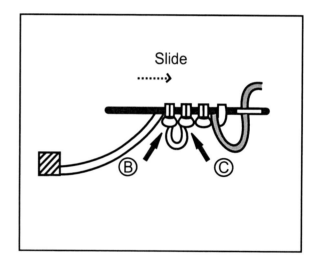

Slide

Picot Gauge

A picot gauge measures the size of picots. Using the same gauge on all picots creates same sized picots.

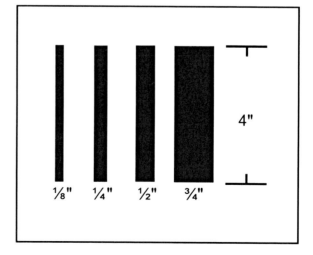

⅛"   ¼"   ½"   ¾"   4"

Picot gauges may be made from an empty cereal box, the back of a yellow legal pad, or the back of a used school notebook.

Cut gauge to size ⅛" x 4", ¼" x 4", ½" x 4", ¾" x 4".

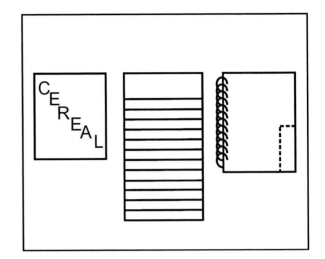

[A] Insert picot gauge flush against front of the needle and next to last double stitch. Firmly pull Ball Thread over picot gauge.

Between right thumb and index finger, pinch the picot gauge, Ball Thread, and the needle at the same time.

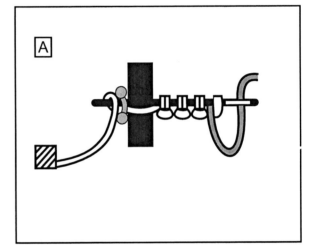

[B] Make First Half Stitch. Snug it up against the picot gauge. Hold First Half Stitch in the pinch.

Then make Second Half Stitch and snug it up against First Half Stitch.

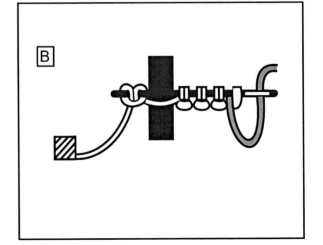

C Remove picot gauge.

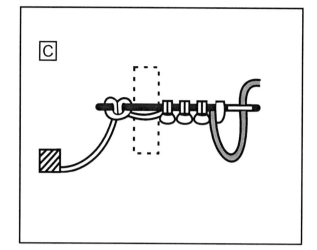

D Slide new double stitch next to previous double stitch. Bare Thread Space creates a picot.

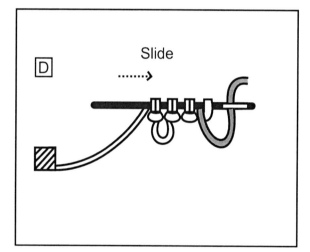

Pinch

Pinch thread or other object(s) between thumb and index finger.

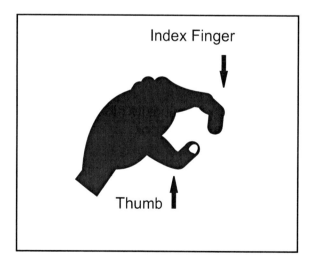

A Reverse Order of Double Stitch(es) (RODS):

1 Make counterclockwise wrap.

2 Bend index finger. Insert needle toward fingernail. Lift thread on to needle.

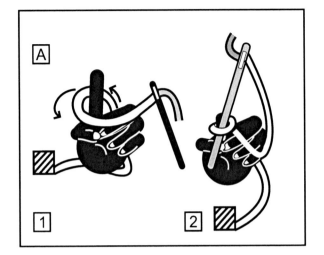

B Make clockwise wrap. Lift thread on to needle. Snug up double stitch.

Make double stitches in reverse order by repeating A and B as many times as required by the pattern instructions.

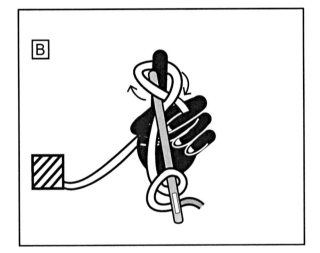

Reverse Work (RW):

Flip lace to its opposite side as if opening an oven door.

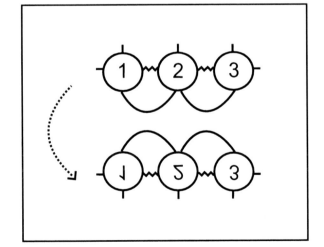

Reverse Work: Reference Point

The method (reverse work, turn work, or rotate) used to set up for next element depends on the reference point. The last completed element is the reference point. You can rotate, reverse, or turn work (e.g., ring) to get in position to make the next element (e.g., chain).

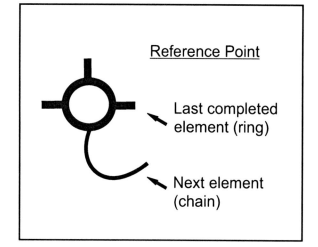

Reference Point

Last completed element (ring)

Next element (chain)

Rotate Work (Rtt)

Turn lace like a bicycle wheel spins. (Do not turn lace to its opposite side.)

You can spin your work in a clockwise or counterclockwise direction.

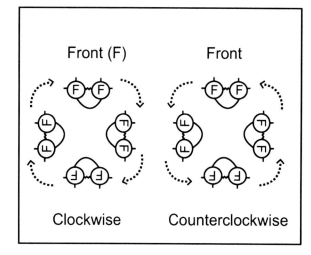

Front (F)   Front

Clockwise   Counterclockwise

Round (Rnd)

A round is a <u>completed</u> pattern sequence. (For pattern abbreviations see page 60.)

Example: Ring-Chain Pattern

Rnd 1: (1st pattern sequence)
<u>Ring:</u> 3 ds, p, 3 ds, p, 3 ds, p, 3 ds. Cl. TW.
<u>Chain:</u> 8 ds. Cl. TW.

Rnd 2: (2nd pattern sequence)
<u>Ring:</u> 3 ds, p, 3 ds, p, 3 ds, p, 3 ds. Cl. TW.
<u>Chain:</u> 8 ds. Cl. TW.

First round = ring and chain.
Second round = repeated ring and chain.

To create a third round, add another ring and chain (in other words, add one more complete pattern sequence).

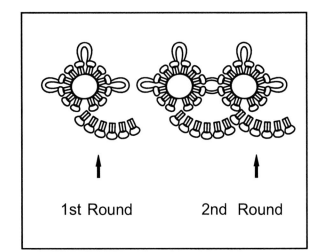

1st Round   2nd Round

How many rounds are in this illustration? ➡

The second figure cannot be counted as a round because it lacks a chain. The Ring-Chain Pattern sequence should include both a ring and a chain to be complete.

(Answer: 1)

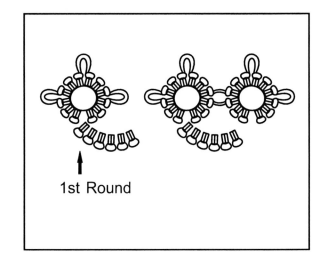

1st Round

Round and ± :

− = in the first round there is no join to the picot.

+ = in the second round a new picot joins to the old picot.

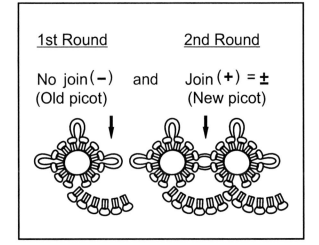

1st Round   2nd Round

No join (−)   and   Join (+) = ±
(Old picot)   (New picot)

Round or Row (Additional definition):

When the first element Ⓐ (composed of three rings in this pattern: one large and two small) and last element Ⓙ (chain) are joined, this completes a round.

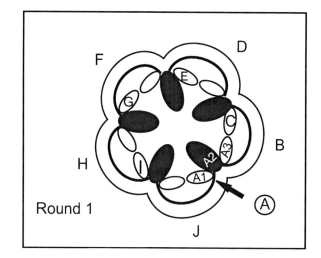

Round 1

The new row is identified as Round 2 in pattern instructions.

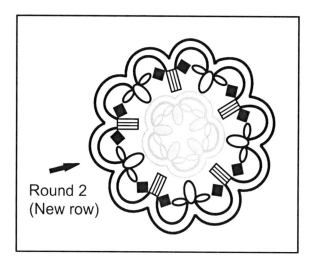

Round 2
(New row)

Sew in Tail Ends

Before cutting Ball Thread (BT) and Needle Thread (NT), leave 6" tails. Tie tails in a square knot (◆) (see page 52).

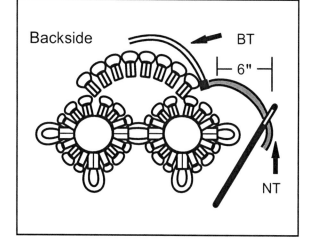

Backside

49

A *Unthread needle. Insert needle (eye first) under three double stitches of chain.

B Rethread needle with Needle Thread. Pull Needle Thread through those three double stitches.*

Repeat once from * to *.

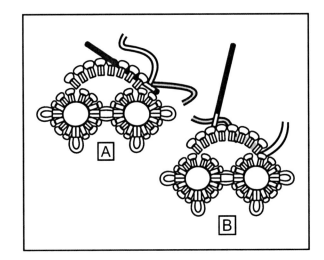

A When completed, Needle Thread tail end is covered by six double stitches.

B Cut off excess Needle Thread.

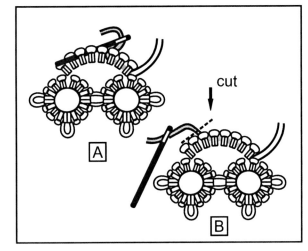

For Ball Thread tail end, repeat twice from * to * above.

A Except insert needle through a different element (e.g., ring).

B White thread represents ball thread hidden <u>beneath</u> double stitches.

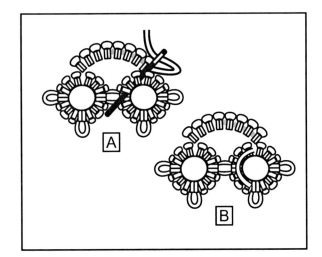

How to Needle Tat

[A] Shoelace Trick (SLT)

SLT is used to close rings and chains. Place Needle Thread (NT) over Ball Thread (BT).

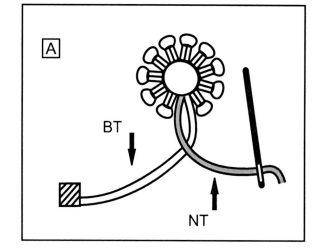

[B] Insert needle under (U) Ball Thread, and through almond shape.

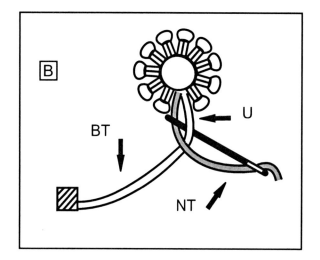

[C] Then insert needle over (O) Ball Thread. Firmly pull on Needle Thread to snug up knot.

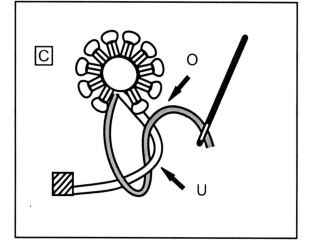

Slip Knot

A Lay Ball Thread on a table in a circular shape. Tail is laid over (O) Ball Thread.

B Weave tail under (U), then over (O) Loop 1. This creates Loop 2.

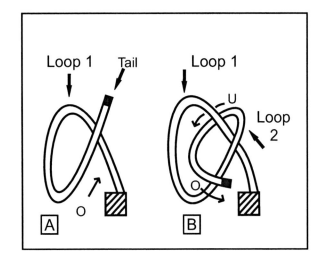

C Weave tail under (U), then over (O) Loop 2.

D Firmly hold tail and Ball Thread in one hand. With opposite hand, insert finger through Loop 1 and pull up loop to tighten.

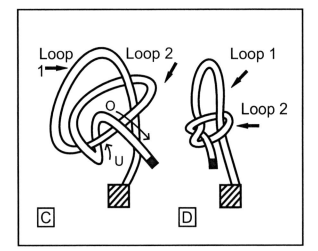

Square Knot (SqK)

Hold one tail end of thread Ⓐ in right hand.

Lay thread Ⓑ on table in semi-circle.

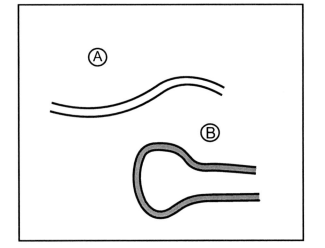

Pick up one tail end of Ⓐ, weave it through Ⓑ in the following manner:

1. Over, 2. Under, 3. Over,
4. Under, 5, Over, 6. Under

O = Over   U = Under

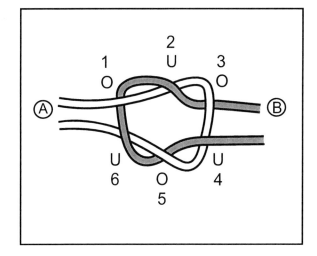

1 Hold ends Ⓐ & Ⓑ in left hand.

2 Hold ends Ⓒ & Ⓓ in right hand.

3 Pull hands in opposite directions to tighten square knot.

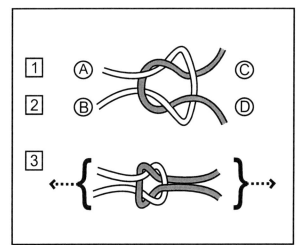

Turn Work (TW):

Turn work to its opposite side as if turning a page in a book.

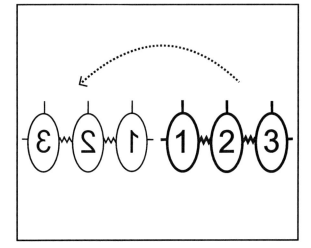

How to Make and Use a Pinning Board	

T-Pins (1 box)	
Spray Starch (1 can)	
Waxed Paper	WAXED PAPER
Cardboard Box	
Cut out 12" x 10" piece of cardboard	12" x 10"
Tissues	Tissue
Tear off two 10.5" x 11.9" pieces of waxed paper	10.5" x 11.9"

Pin first piece of wax paper to cardboard.

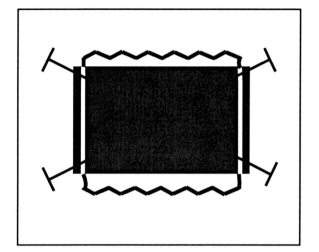

Lay lace on top of second piece of waxed paper.

In a well ventilated area, spray starch on front side. Turn over lace. Spray starch on backside. Lace should be completely soaked with starch. Use tissue to dab off excess starch.

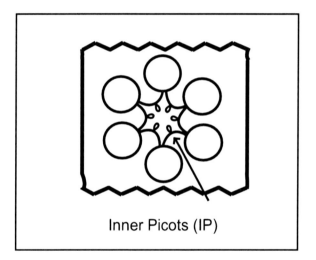

Inner Picots (IP)

Place wet lace on first piece of waxed paper. Smooth lace with hand until it lays flat against the waxed paper. Pin inner picots open.

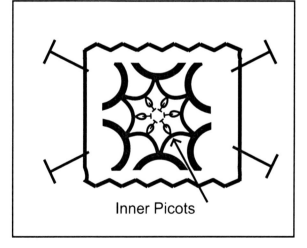

Inner Picots

Order of Pinning

Place pin on north side of tatting (1), smooth lace flat with left hand, then pin south side of tatting (2). As you pin, keep alternating between opposite sides of lace.

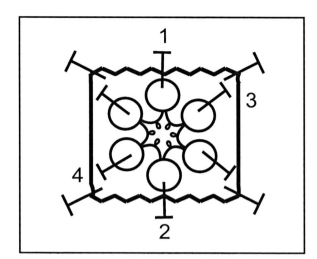

Finishing Tatted Lace

If you have used high quality thread, then picots should be open. However, if picots are closed or twisted or lace doesn't lay flat, then it is necessary to use a pinning board.

You can buy spray starch at your local grocery or craft store. Or use one of the following alternative methods to finish the lace. The method used depends on the purpose of the lace.

Distilled Water

Use this method for heirloom lace intended to be handed down from generation to generation. Do not use starch. Starch will, over time, deteriorate the thread.

Place lace in a clean container. For large pieces of lace such as curtains, place lace in a clean bathtub.

Clean Container:

Pour in enough distilled water to cover tatting. Gently press down on tatting to completely immerse it in the water. Do not stir or agitate tatting. You may gently swish the water. Let lace soak about 10 minutes to one hour in room temperature distilled water. Allow more time to soak if tatting is extremely soiled.

To remove lace from water: Do not twist or wring lace. Do not pull lace out of water. These actions will weaken the threads.

Remove lace by placing a hand, fingers spread over top of container. Gently pour out all water. Place container above clean towel(s). "Pour" lace on top of towel. Straighten lace so it lays flat on the towel. Then roll up towel to soak up excess water. Transfer lace to a second dry towel. Roll it up to soak up excess water. If

56

necessary, repeat this process. Then pin on pinning board. Let it dry.

Clean Bathtub:

Lace should lay equally distributed across bottom of the tub. Pour distilled water over lace until it is completely covered. Let lace soak for at least 20 minutes, longer if lace is extremely soiled.

Before removing lace, have several clean towels ready. Then place your hand on the lace, preventing it from touching the drain. Open drain and let water out. Place clean towels on top of lace to soak up remaining water. Gently lift lace out of tub. Lay lace on top of several clean, dry, flat towels. Roll up towels to soak up excess water. Transfer lace to a new set of dry towels. Shape lace so that picots are open and lace lays flat.

Homemade Starch

Stir 1/4 cup cornstarch into one cup of tepid water. Keep stirring until cornstarch is dissolved.

Add this mixture to a quart of water in a pan. Place pan on a burner. Turn stove burner to high. Stir this mixture until it comes to a boil. Remove pan. Turn off burner.

Heavy Starch: Use mixture as it is. Make sure it has cooled down to a warm temperature. Use heavy starch when lace needs to be very stiff.

Medium Starch: Pour 1 quart of cold water in pan and stir.

Light Starch: Add 2 quarts of cold water to pan and stir. Use light starch when lace needs a little bit of drape such as a shawl.

Sugar and Water

Use this recipe when lace takes a 3-D shape such as a bell. After applying mixture to bell, mold bell on a rounded form to dry.

Use a one-to-one ratio when mixing sugar and water. Melt 1/2 cup sugar and 1/2 cup water together in a pan over medium heat. Constantly stir until mixture is clear. Let mixture cool until it is warm. Immediately use this mixture while it is still warm.

If you wait too long, the cool mixture will be unevenly soaked up. This gives the lace an uneven color when it dries.

Elmer's Glue

This method is best used with greeting cards. Lay lace on waxed paper. With a sponge apply glue mixture to both sides of lace. Use a tissue to wipe off any excess glue. Transfer lace to clean piece of waxed paper. Shape lace so picots are open and it lays flat. Keeping its shape, gently lift lace off of waxed paper and place on greeting card. Let it dry. It is automatically glued to the card.

Glue Mixture

Dilute glue with enough distilled water to produce a runny consistency like milk. It should flow easily over the lace. Approximate measurements are one tablespoon of Elmer's Glue mixed with two tablespoons of distilled water.

Why I learned to Tat

Betsy was 91 years old when I first met her. She grew up and lived most of her life in the same rural Nebraska town. In 1920, she became a farmer's wife when she married her first husband. In 1941, after surviving the Great Depression, her husband died of an undiagnosed illness.

During WWII Betsy moved to Omaha. Then, in 1958, she married another farmer from her hometown. Back on a farm, she raised a garden to help feed her family. She had a family of five which included three children.

Among all the cares of raising a family and helping out on a farm, she was able to maintain her interest in fishing. She must have passed this interest on to her son. He became a researcher. For a time, he lived in the Galapagos Islands and studied those 800-plus-pound turtles.

Another of Betsy's interests was tatted lace. For our Annual Bazaar at church, she donated several sets of tatted notecards. The cards were made from copy paper, folded into quarters. She used a single strand of embroidery floss to make tatted flowers. She glued four to six flowers to a card. Beneath the flowers, in green ink, she drew lovely stems and leaves.

Every year at Annual Bazaar, her cards consistently sold out. Ladies would rush to snap them up. Every year I, too, looked forward to replenishing my supply of tatted note cards. For nine years, I maintained this purchasing habit. Then, at age 100, Betsy died.

I didn't notice the conspicuous absence of tatted cards at Annual Bazaar until the year after she died. Betsy was the only tatter in our church. There would be no more tatted cards unless I learned how to make them.

I began my search for a tatting teacher. When I asked around town, I found no one in our small town knew how to tat.

Then I asked people from a neighboring small town. I found one lady in her eighties. She had been tatting for many years. One day, for about an hour, I sat and watched her tat. She moved her shuttle very quickly—nearly a blur. When I returned home, I brought some books and finished teaching myself to tat.

Tatted lace is a beautiful art and worth preserving. Beauty is a treasure rarely noted in a nightly news report. There are many storms in life. A few minutes spent tatting is a refuge—a relaxing remnant of a gentle era.

Thank you for your interest in tatted lace. I wish you many pleasurable hours of tatting.

Laura

Be the first to know about available new patterns. Go to: www.abctattingpatterns.com.

Abbreviation Key

Ball Thread	= BT
Bare Thread Space	= BTS
Chain	= Ch or ⌣
Clockwise Wrap	= CW
Close	= Cl
Counterclockwise Wrap	= CCW
Cut and Tie thread tails	= C&T
Double Stitch(es)	= DS
Flawless Front	= FF
First Half Stitch	= 1HS
Second Half Stitch	= 2HS
Index Finger	= Ⓘ
Join	= J / + / ± / ∿
Josephine Chain (or Spiral)	= JC / JS
Josephine Knot	= JK
Left Hand	= LH
Middle Finger	= Ⓜ
Mock Picot	= MP / ☒
Needle Thread	= NT
Over	= O
Picot	= P / — / ◊
Pinch	= ●━●
Pinky Finger	= Ⓟ
Reverse Order of DS	= RODS
Reverse Work	= RW
Right Hand	= RH
Ring	= R / ○
Ring Finger	= Ⓡ
Rotate Work	= Rtt
Shoe Lace Trick	= SLT
Split Chain	= S/C
Split Ring	= S/R
Square Knot	= SqK / ◆
Thumb	= Ⓣ
Turn Work	= TW
Under	= U
Very Small Picot (⅛")	= VSP / ∧

CPSIA information can be obtained at www.ICGtesting.com
Printed in the USA
BVOW03s2112040716

453897BV00025B/71/P